FALLOW FURROW

Written by:

Ngozi Olivia Osuoha

Edited by:

Jerry Langdon

Printed by:
Raven Cage Publishing and Amazon KPD

First Printing Edition, 2022
ISBN 9798841192435

Table of Contents

THE FEMALE FOLKS

The world cannot grow in any form
If she decides to have women deformed,
The earth cannot rotate or perform
If it keeps females uninformed.

The female folk is a propeller
A great and unthinkable controller,
Marching and matching things aright
Ticking and tracking issues with might.

The pole is not our role
Our sole is not a hole.

The girl child is a boom
The woman is a glow
The female has the flow,
The world cannot do without her.

Care, love, build and rebuild
Affection, attention, passion and motivation
Give women the room!

POETS OF THE YEARS

I am a poet, I write poems and prose
I am a writer, I write hymns and essays
I am an inker, I ink in and out
I am a thinker, I think up and down.

Year after year, I have been writing long ago
Poets dance with pen
They enjoy the rhythm and the flow
Crack your head, rock your mind
Poets tear up on paper.

Pen and paper, ink and paint
We are artists, we are painters
We sing, we pray, we preach
Poets are deities, they dare the odds!

Weeks, months, years and decades
Seconds, minutes, hours, days and lifetime;
Poets, we are! Poets of the time!

I LOVE YOU

My heart is large for you
Warm, green and pure to live
My soul is clean for you
Wide, free and fair to love.

Live in my mind and spirit
Play, pray and party at will
My arms are great and rich
Let my love guide you beyond.

I love you, now and then
Keep your heart free for me
Dance and hug my eager spirit
For my passion is burning anew!

HOLY DOVE

Wilder, we are going
Wider, we are burning
Weirder, we are crushing
Cracking, crumbling and wobbling
Come, holy dove
Return with magnitudes of peace!

Holy dove, return
This urn is burning down
Spread your precious apparel of peace,
Let the sons of men wear it in unity!

Holy dove, dove divine
Celestial mystery of serenity
Drive homeward, speed forth your tranquil
Cause this chaos to chill!

Roll away sorrow and pain
Wrap up cruelty and hate
Sweep off inhumanity
Fold back this insanity,
Holy dove, dove pure and sure
Sanctify the world again and forever!

LOVE IS THE GREATEST

Love yourself, and live right
Love your neighbour and protect them
For we pass away in a moment.

Love conquers hate and greed
It is not selfish, it is not arrogant
Shine through the gloom
And let the world blossom.

Come, let's play together
Instead of the war, killing ourselves
Come, let's live together
Rather than the terror, harming one another.

We can be at peace, yes, we can
For only but a moment we live
And only in a moment we are gone.

DON'T LOOK FOR TROUBLE

Don't look for trouble, it has tentacles
And brews numerous obstacles,
Don't look for trouble, it grows jungles
And performs no miracles.

Don't look for trouble, some trouble have multiple effects
And cause harms and defects
Don't look for trouble, they will not spare you
Rather pour you tars, and weed you like tares.

Look up to your journey
And head for your destination,
March on to the future
And let the world hear you rupture!

Again, I say to you, don't look for trouble
For trouble troubles he who troubles trouble.

I AM NOT A FOOL

I fall down, deep down below, rolling still down
Gathering dust and dirt from the ground
You laugh and merry, thinking I am a fool,
I am not a fool!

You manipulate, manoeuvre and mastermind misery
Believing you are on the fast lane to wealth and affluence
Hey you! Think not I am fool!

Sometimes, I turn a blind eye
Other times, I borrow a deaf ear
Those times, I learn a dumb lip
Most times, I ponder how you betray
Many a time, I wonder how you lie
Much ado, you thunder why you blunder
While my whole being quake at your yonder.

I am not a fool, I wait, I pray you redress
I hope you repent, because I fear your end.

Do not abuse respect, or humility
Never outsmart trust, or honesty
For transparency is not weakness Neither are ignorance,
innocence, vulnerability, ability and capability what you think!

PRIDE

Ego is a cloak, it hinders proper sight
Chop it off, and let it go!

Pride is a thorn, it cracks your horn
So swipe and wipe away the dirty pipe.

The king does not need introduction
Because his kingdom reigns in all the realms.

The shepherd may not be in robe
But he surely knows his scope.

Pride can kill and break the windmill
Side by side, divide and hide;
One is sold, and told to hold.

Submit, tender the bender and render the sender
Admit, hail the nail for it not to wail.

Vulnerable people can be honourable
Honourable people can be vulnerable,
Venerable, charitable, admirable
Sensible, humble and able
One is not forced to cross the boundary.

SEARCHING FOR REST

I have been here singing this song of pain
Trying to understand why the world is cruel and life unfair,
But it seems I sink deeper into void and emptiness.

My voice picks high notes and transcends into low frequencies
Yet, I cannot hear myself.

Why would my soul thirst for peace and yet find war
As if I am a warrior?
Why would I hope for joy and bottle up sadness in my spirit
As though I am a beast?

Friends turn down my hand, and partners crush my love
Yet my body ages as though I make progress.

In life, what else could be more fulfilling if not unity and peace,
Could death bring growth?

Heathens rage, the earthen vessels break
Breakfasts spill, lunch freeze, and dinner sour,
How can my soul then find rest?

Daily I long and search for rest
Still my nest become a pest and my best turn jest, dipping into my crest zest.
Shady, rocky, deadly, heady, sloppy,
Then I ask who makes headway in muddy waters?

THE MONSTER AND BEAST

Here comes the monster
Crawling like a lobster
In a huge cluster
Booming like a youngster.

See him in green strength
Teeming at full length,
Yet he is a beast
Setting the sun in the east.

Raping every breast
Cutting bare their chest,
Forcing them to the west
And stealing their rest.

In little circles and clusters
They become tyrants
In small groups and fosters
They eat up our elephants.

Rest is far from me
Hope flies away
Joy wonders aloof
Happiness deserts my land,
Yet they call me blessed.

These monsters cage me in agony
And these beasts take advantage of me,

I am wet with pain
And watered in anger,
Fear sings loud against me
Tear and wear patch my life
Who has not heard me cry?

Loud and constant, I wail
Weeping to be consoled.

Hitherto, I mourn, mourning even in the morning
Moreso, I am nice, even at noon
Thereto, I knit, knitting like a knight at night
My mouth, my knee, my sight, all shake and quake, sharing in
quarantine
And yet this rest doesn't want to come!

WE MADE IT

Of the hurdles and puzzles
In the midst of scarcity,
Of the deaths and accidents
In the midst of life and love,
Of the pains and stains
In the midst of fears and tears,
Wow! We made it!

Traumas and dramas
Stigmas and dilemmas
Hammers and failures,
Oh, we made it!

Sicknesses and diseases
Epidemics and pandemics
Shutdowns and lockdowns
Meltdowns and recessions
O dear friends, we made it!

Happy new year, happy world
I wish us well, better and stronger
Happy new year, dear world
I wish us safety, love and peace.

A NEW WORLD

The past is gone behind us
Yes, let's leave it there and move on
The year is spent, gone forever
It will never come, come to haunt us.

Leave it behind, move on
Let it go, focus on the future
It's a new year, let's dance ahead
Whatever happened, let it go!

We can live better and happy
Yes, we can be stronger and livelier
If we choose to turn a new leaf.

Happy new year, happy new year
We conquered the troubles
We subdued the years,
Come on, it's a new year
Don't limit it to mere resolutions
Because all things are possible.

Dust yourself, clean your coat
Wear your shoes, guard your loins
We made it, it's a new year
We could make it a new world.

May the heavens smile on us
May the stars light our paths

May the moon never cease to give us joy
May the sun keep shining and smiling on us
May the universe favour us continually
Hip! Hip! Hip! Hurray!!

I WILL NEVER SEND THIS LETTER

You were so gorgeous like a king
Sparking like a knight in shining armour
Your crown dazzled with diamonds
And your staff stood like a pillar,
So I fell for you like a pack of cards.

You were everything that I ever wanted
I dreamed so long that you became real
The sole of your feet was a bridge
It crossed me between borders and shores,
But you were a stinking sinking ship.

The apparel of angels you wore
But the garment of saints, you tore
Ungodliness was your robe
And worldliness your wardrobe,
Yet you glitter like gold.

Trusting you was my crime
Loving you was my evil
And accepting you was my downfall.

I didn't pray for agony
I don't wish to reap sorrow
Rather I hope for the best,
Hence I'll never send this letter.

MY WORLD

Someday, I'm gonna fly
High, on top the sky
My wings would be dry
And I'm not gonna cry,
Because I wouldn't be wet
So won't be pulled by weight.

Someday, I would take off
Flying without a cuff
Healthy lungs devoid of cough
Wealthy soul that's enough,
Lengthy life full of energy
Soothing milk without allergy.

Yes, my wings bud
Despite the mud
My wings grow
Despite the stings
Yes, I'm reaching for the space.

My world, green and blue
After the black and white,
My world, bright and beautiful
After the pale and veil
My world, great and wonderful
After the horror and sorrow.

I'm reaching for the space

To win my race
Up I lift my face
Guided by grace,
I am taking my place
Divinely at pace.

ENDS OF THE EARTH

I wake up and wail as I ponder
Crying to understand what life is all about
Yet I find little or no answer
As I get lost.

Under the shadow of trees, I am not free
 Yonder the window of doubts I try to sprout
  Beyond I reach to teach but within ditch.

Upon the ends of the earth, I run
I grab voices to shout aloud
 I borrow noises to ring the alarm
  hearken dear earth upon my homeward way.

From the ends of the earth I mourn
 Seeking peace and love to live
  consoling myself shamefully in pain,
   Lo, here pegs the lungs of a child
    a child buried amidst life and plenty because he was hated.

IF I RULED YOU

Give me your neck let me strangle you
 so that you would know I am your ruler,
  and a tormentor.

If I ruled you, you wouldn't breathe
 because I would deprive you of air and nostrils,
  I would blind your eyes and shut your mind
   you know I am your ruler.

I would skin you alive and butcher you
just give me a chance, you would like it,
 this life you live is uncalled for, you dare not.

If I ruled you, I would vomit on you
 that way I would be the lord and king,
If I ruled you, no need for your voice nor word.

JEZEBEL

Jezebel, got married to Abel
She built a brothel for citadel
And he raised an altar to alter all.

Jezebel stole a holy pole
And her pole was a hole,
Abel, a Fidel in whole
He sacrificed and was sanctified.

Jezebel, the plotter and rioter
Destroyer and spoiler,
Abel, the cleaner and teacher
Learner and lifter.

Jezebel, a coiled cobra
Abel, an able army
Parallel, opposite and unlike
Both, in a forced marriage.

WE ARE THE WORLD

We are the world
We live in heaven or hell
We are the world
We live or die.

We support injustice and greed
We buttress selfishness and violence,
We are the world
We do so directly or indirectly.

We preach love but live hate
We sing hymns but drop bombs,
We dance blues but play war,
We are the world
We sink yonder.

Look, we pretend a lot
And cover evil
We coat lies
And bury truths,
See, we are crooks.

We are the world
Except we face realities
Until we become real
Unless we decide to grow
This world would remain hell.

We ink, we drum, we act, we play
We sing, we pray, we party, all in hell
This doom booms
And the gloom, looms
Heed, we are the world
Let us make it a better place.

DEAR FRIEND

Greetings my dear friend
I hope you are in peace
I am no longer comfortable
I feel unsafe and worried
Hence I write you this letter.

I fear your silence is loud
Your negligence is so obvious
You no longer care nor love
And the loneliness is killing me.

Today you are on
Tomorrow you are off
On and off, off and on
I do not know your stand again
So I cannot boast you still love me.

Please tell me you are for real
Let me know you are alive
That you have not gone like others
O my dear friend,
This is not friendship anymore
Because in the beginning, it was not so.

MY COUNTRY

Come, cry for me
For I am troubled, so troubled
Come, cry with me
For I am in pain, so pained,
Painted, fainted, a dirty painting
A fainting that is draining me.

My country burns, burning in flames
My homeland mourns, mourning in shame
My fatherland is quaking
Quaking loud and aloud
Shaking the cloud and crowd.

Pray for me please, please I pray thee
My land bleeds in greed
Lives waste in hundreds
Tears overflow daily
Fears gather amidst
Nothing, nobody is safe,
Please pray for me, my people, and my country.

IN THE WINGS OF VIOLENCE

Hear the wind rage
See the rain raging
The thunder strikes
Lightning gives horror
My people are swept over.

In the wings of violence
My land encroaches to war
Fighting, killing, maiming, raping
Hear war sing freely to us.

In the wings of violence
I hear innocence moan,
In the wings of terror
I see generations groan
Look deep and yonder
Leadership is terrorism.

Religion has beheaded us
Politics has bewitched us
Hatred, falsehood, fallacy, dogmatism
Hey! I fear now and tomorrow!

COLD WAR

We are at war
We are barely alive
They pounce on us raw
We are halfway dead.

A cold war so loud
The world is busy
So busy that we are insignificant.

The world is on
On, ongoing with activities
The world is on its wings
As we oscillate on swings.

Leadership is no more fair
Friendship is now a nightmare
Partnership is cruelty
Relationship is wickedness,
The world looks the other way,
As we dive and plunge into the abyss
Head on collision with death.

A cold war, within and without
Gold, hold, sold, fold, told and untold.

THE FOOLISH MAJORITY

Illiterate men on rampage
Garnering raw courage,
Rolling in ignorance
Causing huge nuisance.

Wayward women on gear
Speeding without fear,
Jerking at random
Wishing for stardom.

The foolish majority
Rising against the minority,
Riding on the wings of gang-up
Sliding through frame-up.

Uncultured, unmannered, untrained
Insincere, inhumane, insane
Free for all, abusive
Uncoordinated, unconstitutional, repulsive.

See them in kinsmen
Amidst brotherhood,
See them in semen
Amidst neighborhood.

The foolish majority
A family of bandits,
The portable entity

A family of dirty habits.

They have a goal
So dark like charcoal,
They dig coal
Just to burn up truths.

They steal dowries
And sell cowries,
They swallow moons
And swear by noons.

FAR FROM THE MADDING CROWD

When you are far from the madding crowd
They think you are possessed,
When you are far from the madding crowd
They call you a witch.

They call you names
To cover their games,
They paint you black
To gather their back.

See, look, listen, and hear
They live in darkness
Staggering in hate
And swerving in bitterness,
They hire mates to lay siege.

When you are far from the madding crowd
By being sane and sound,
They cook diverse holes in whole
Just to scatter and shatter.

They block and mount roadblocks
They are snipers and whisperers,
Shooting, and murmuring
Looting, and devouring.

They are evildoers
Doing wrong, piling up insanity,

Divers of ugly trends
 Trending horror and terror.

They gather for evil
They backbite, gossip and blackmail
Scandals give them blood
Slandering and defamation inspire them
Character assassination is their sole aim,
They jubilate over crimes they perform
And celebrate their atrocities.

 Far from the madding crowd, heroes are
Giants become ashes by these foilers
 Legends turn crazy from them; toilers
 So the foolish majority sound like thunders
 Instigating, inciting, indicting
But a day of reckoning is coming,
 Let them not cry foul when visited.
SCOTLAND

Scotland, the beautiful bride
Come take me on a walk
Fly me high and far
Teach me wonders of love.

Scotland, my green love
Take me to the Queen
I want to see the palace
And feel the warmness of royalty.

Scotland, my dear friend

I want to write you a letter,
I hope you would reply
Because I care to be with you.

Scotland, the Scottish Lord
Your kings are unique,
Your princes, spectacular
Your knights shine amazing
You are so blessed a people.

Clean and neat you are
Pure and great you grow
Sane and sound your land
Grown and matured your features.

TWELFTH NIGHT

See how beautiful you are
Green, red, yellow, blue and pink
Purple, brown, orange, indigo and violet
Sparking colours of rainbow
Chasing away gloom and danger.

The meadows and the greenwoods
The plantations and the gardens
The vegetations and the shrubs
The mountains and the valleys
The thorns and the roses
The trees and the flowers
The summer and the winter
The autumn and the spring
The breezes, the dews, the fogs, the mists, the snow
All nature, all real, all great.

Tales by moonlight, stars shooting and resting
Wonders unfolding, Scotland, Scot and Scottish
Your men dress gorgeous
Your women dress like goddesses
O Scotland of Macbeth
Precious land of Shakespeare
Home of heroes and legends
Place of adventures and tales
History keeps writing beyond the twelfth night.

MY GUARDIAN ANGEL

True love from above
Flying like a dove
Divine wings
Holy rings,
Spreading purity and trinity.

My real hero
Lifting me from zero
My pure strength
Guarding me at length.

Dependable and reliable
Capable and able,
Holding me down
Cleaning my gown.

My guardian angel
My golden apparel,
My Knight in shining armour
My light in dark humour.

Lily in my valley
Family of my belly
My ally, my alloy, my envoy
Guiding me through the convoy.

Respectful, honest, decent
Godly, homely, humble

Lovely, lowly, my heart;
We can start any art.

-34-

WE ARE THE WORLD

We are the world
We live in heaven or hell
We are the world
We live or die.

We support injustice and greed
We buttress selfishness and violence,
We are the world
We do so directly or indirectly.

We preach love but live hate
We sing hymns but drop bombs,
We dance blues but play war,
We are the world
We sink yonder.

Look, we pretend a lot
And cover evil
We coat lies
And bury truths,
See, we are crooks.

We are the world
Except we face realities
Until we become real
Unless we decide to grow
This world would remain hell.

We ink, we drum, we act, we play
We sing, we pray, we party, all in hell
This doom booms
And the gloom, looms
Heed, we are the world
Let us make it a better place.

MYSTERY

I wonder deep and get lost
As I wander far and via off
I derail and fail down the rail
Moving slowly like the snail
Yet get soaked in the rain of pain.

I cannot comprehend life
Events torment me to the bones
Circumstances drill me dry
Situations drag me in the mud
Conditions pull my muscles
I cry in fear and weep in wear
As mysteries throw us up and down.

Morals have become traps
Principles have turn delays
Self-discipline is now a grave
And self-control a disqualification,
I don't understand life
I can't comprehend mysteries
People take advantage of the meek.

No wonder majority follow the bandwagon
No wonder they turn a madding crowd
And create animal kingdoms
If that would take them to stardom
Or cure their boredom.

Help me, hold my hand
Let my head not covered in sand
Nor my face buried in shame
Let my feet aright, alright, rightly stand.

AFTER THE WAR

Was it not yesterday that they struck
And got our corpses loaded in their truck
Dragged our lifeless bodies along valleys
And poured our wasted souls into gullies,
See them, parade in victory.

After the war, they never ceased
Rather they seized every opportunity to kill
Hear them till graves and shallow tombs
Annihilation, marginalization, extermination.

Soldiers, aids, uniforms in concord
A discourse and concourse
Envoy, convoy and voyage
Blood, flooding the carnage.

After the war, they held on
Horrors in pieces and bits
Terrors on nieces and kits
Watch, listen, hear them rage louder!

We rise, yes we do, the muse
For the rising sun only sets with nature
Rains, clouds, nights and days
Dews, mist, moist, fog, they all gear.

Blood rise in wells
As they ring like bells

Calling forth for peace
Singing songs of love
Writing books of unity
Saying words of progress
Gathering dust of justice
Yet after the war, the pogroms return.

Genocides, homicides, afflictions
Hate, hate upon hate
War, war after war
Call a dog a bad name
And have it publicly beheaded for festival.

In memory of those killed during the Biafran war

WHEN GREEN IS RED

Green is life, it is fertile
Green is growth, it is development
Green is pure, it is sanity
Green is great, it is sanctity
But green has turned red, here.

Green is alife, it lives forever
Green is afloat, it stays evergreen
But in my land, green is red.

Blood is flowing, nooks and crannies
Blood is the Latin, praying in our mountain,
And it is now the fountain we drink.

CATASTROPHE

They are all catalysts
Showing on catalogs,
They are all caterpillars
Destroying our pillars,
Catalogs of catastrophes
Catastrophic catalogs
Carting away our corridors
Escalating pungent odours
Agents of accidents in porous aura,
Bunch of cankerworms
A lunch of cancers
Ticking time to bomb
And digging clime as tomb,
Canticles of ill fate
And litanies of wrong faith;
They all are aloof and lost
Running helter skelter
Looking for a shield,
But destruction looms around them.

A WORLD OF WOMEN

They say it's a man's world
So women should not be loud
They forget it is a crowd
Anybody can be loud in the cloud.

We live together, both men and women
We die alike, both male and female
So why not live in peace
And fight to increase?

Live and let live
Do not create a hive
Where bees sting,
Rather build a nest where birds sing.

Give it to women
Protect the girl child,
Give it to humanity
And cure the world's insanity.

We can grow
We can blow
We can glow
We can show
If we don't borrow
We won't sorrow.

Celebrate our women today

Celebrate them tomorrow
Love, be kind
Lead, be gentle
Bless, do not curse
Happy women's day to the globe.

NOBLEST!!

Gentle soul of rare breed
With battle creed along life
Rowing steadily and slowly
With speeding deeds and actions.

Noble, humble, calm and clean
Coordinated, courageous, composed and comported
Kindhearted, considerate, and sensitive
Noble Raji, Noble Ade.

Rising from the dust, climbing to the top
Fighting, focusing and forging ahead
Determined, dedicated, dutiful and decisive.

Noble fellow, noblest of them all
Young, green at heart, the greenest.

Rule the world, reign, you are noble
Sing like a bird, fly and soar
For the earth can never clip the wings of an eagle!
BRAVO DEAR BOSS!

A new height is not a joke
You could have ran from some choke
Yet we may not have heard when you spoke!

A new crown could have some thorns
But we see only the horns,

May everything you have sworn
Never have your heart ever torn.

This ladder is getting higher
These feet are getting stronger,
Up, upper you climb
May you never dash limb.

Boss, the bravo, bravo!
Boss, dear boss, congratulations!
Hip! Hip!! Hurray!!!

A DEEP LITTLE PIECE

Do not flirt with those who can flip you,
Do not crush on those who can crush you.

Flirt not with people lest they flip you,
 Crush not on people lest they crush you.

 Dreams are not realities
Realities are neither dreams,
However, realities could be dreams.

Remember, slow seems the time
But steady ticks the hands,
And none dares stop,
For what will be will be
Because what is written is written.

LET IT RAIN

Showers of blessing
Showers of peace
Showers of healing,
Rain, and cleanse the land.

Rain, spirit supreme
Rain, saviour superior
Reign within forever
Reign without everlasting.

Rain mightily
Rain thunderously
Reign tremendously
Reign jealously.

Rain, flood the earth
Sweep across the crystal sea
Rain, we thirst
Rain, we starve
Please rain, renew us
Rain and revive us
Rain, we perish.

THE LAND OF HOPE

There is a sun in the East
It is fermenting a yeast
To foment and set on a feast,
Because a son in the East
is unleashing his beast.

Eastern heartland;
Plagued like Egypt
Blood flowing like Nile
Turning red, the Niger.

The land of hope
See, cannot cope
For the devilish rope
Has become its scope.

The land of hope
See, is turning hopeless
The Eastern heartland
Look, is becoming a wonderland.

The land of hope
Are you a supreme cult
Or an inferior court,
For I wonder and loss
And my strength misfits the cross.

The land of hope

Watch, I see you become a red sea
A hopeless and helpless mountain
Hear, I mourn for your young men
 I see them waste in vain.

The land of hope
I weep, I wail, I want
I wish, I watch, I waste too
All these make me weak.

The land of hope
A rising sun that wants to set by day
A fading day that gets nothing for the night
Hear me again, I weep and wail
I mourn and melt
I mount upon the altars of our forebears
On the rocks along our way
Upon the chariots of archangels
Speeding forth their flights
Weeding off your foes
Seeding your time and toes
Hoping that you hope aright
And not against hope.

Hear me, men with ears
Listen, let me speak
Spread your wings and seek peace
Lest you pay with your first sons.

Fight with wisdom
Move with intelligence

That ye not give in return all you cherish.

Lead, and lead aright
Follow, and follow aright
See vultures resting on your nests
See ravens waiting for your flesh
Again I come in peace
To warn and warm you of the doom
The wrath of your Creator.

You have drawn swords
See them break
You have built and carved arrows
See them pierce your marrows
Again I mourn for you
I wail and weep for the land
A land hoping, so hopeful yet hopeless
Helplessly destroying itself.

I call on the God of Jacob
And the God of Isaac
And that of Abraham,
The one who chases armies
And crashes Pharaohs
The one who belittles Nebuchadnezzar
And frustrates Ahitophel,
May He descend in mercy.

This land of hope, the eastern heartland
This art on your heart never builds a land
You had better hoped aright,

Make hay while the sun shines
For the land of hope is the eastern heartland,
It needs not be hopeless.

Learn, relearn, unlearn
Recall and never forget history
Lest you live in misery,
For this land of hope in the eastern heartland
Is the rising sun of Mama Africa.

There are Goliaths in Golgotha
There are Davids in Damascus
There are Pauls in Philistine
There are Naomis in Nineveh
There are Esthers in Ethiopia
There are Mordecais in Macedonia
There are Jaels in Jerusalem
There are Joels in Jericho
There are Josephs in Jordan
There are Salomes in Sodom
There are Solomons in Sinai
There are Esaus in Israel
There are Zachariahs in Zion
There are Elijahs in Egypt
I warn again and ask
Who are you in Imo state,
Where are the wise men from the East?

CONSTANT

In life, everyone is important

Though troubles are incessant

Forcing us to lack and want,

Conquerors become triumphant

Losers grow small like an ant

Whether heavy like an elephant.

Soldiers are on and gallant,

Very brave and nonchalant

Neither dull nor redundant

With the zeal of a merchant,

Whether or not he has a chant

He waters his field and plant.

Every model is elegant

He may be an applicant

Better, a real communicant

Though not the only grant,

However, there is a confidant

Who, our relief is a constant.

POOR JESUS, I HOPE YOU ARE NOT A COWARD.

Poor, wretched, you were born in a manger
Into a ridiculous lineage,
With a mysterious paternity
They said by a virgin;
A wonderment.

Animals talk not
So your poor background was safe,
They could not have disturbed you.

The King asked for your head
And you fled,
Cry, cry, baby.

You borrowed money from the fish to pay your tax
You borrowed bread and fish from a boy to feed multitudes,
You borrowed an ox for your triumphant entry,
Borrow, borrow, Jesus.

You spoke in parables
To avoid lynching,
Yet, how did you die?

You took a thief to Paradise
Because of your weakness,
Poor Jesus, I pity you.

You fixed an ear that was cut off

You asked that we turn our right cheek for another slap,
You warned that we cut off any body part that can lead us astray,
Fearful Jesus, are you not a coward?

You answered Pilate indirectly
You asked the mob to stone first if they were innocent,
You allowed a prostitute to anoint you
It was also a prostitute who first saw you resurrect,
Are you really the Redeemer?

You played with children, the vulnerable
Because they could not insult nor beat you,
You were always seeking the other side,
Are you not a coward?

Your mates own planets
And rule worlds
They kill at will
They behead blasphemers
And bomb infidels,
They burn religious places
And maim saints,
Yet, you pray for them
Poor Jesus, that is cowardice.

They even call you gay
They make caricature of you, steadily
They flog, spit, drag and abuse you
You are their cinema
Still, you tarry
Poor Jesus, I hope you are not a coward!

They turned your father's house to a den of robbers
You only chased them away
You had no strength to fight,
Because you are a coward, maybe!

Fear, trembling, doubts, all in you
See, they conduct polls
Polls between you and superstars
Celebrities win, poor Jesus, sorry!

Look, blasphemers punish blasphemers
Madness chase madness
Blindness pursue darkness,
Poor Jesus and you are just there,
Praying, waiting and hoping like a coward.

You are too calm for my liking
Your doctrines baffle me
Your teachings confuse me
Only cowards do things like that,
You even prayed let the cup pass over you,
Jesus, are you not God??

Miracle worker, you charged none
Magicians make fortunes
Powerful healer, only one leper thanked you
Sorcerers receive tithes,
Saviour, who gave his life
Diviners drink blood,
Are you not at loss, poor Jesus?

Look at the crowd
Chanting crucify him, crucify him
They are working for you, your father
Maybe virgin cherubs await them
And spotless seraphs adorn their beds for them!

Poor Jesus, I hope you are not a coward
These fingerings into your eyes are much,
Men scorn your sacred name
Wolves devour your flock and fold,
Arise, arise O morning Star
Arise and never set,
Let these raging heathens see light!

WORKERS' DAY

Kill not the legend in you
That, the hero in you dies not,
Never starve a giant you inhabit
Feed the guru you carry,
Sell not your angel
Even for your head.

For my legend and my hero
For my giant and my guru,
For my angel and my head;
They are me, I am them
Solidarity forever:
For the union makes us strong.

HAPPY WORKERS' DAY

WORKERS' DAY; A FIERY FURNACE FOR PENSIONERS

Without any struggles, horrors, pains, regrets, fears, and doubts a senior citizen should bless God for today, May Day because as a senior citizen, the most memorable holiday should be the Workers' Day, I mean all things being equal...but how are the mighty fallen!

Senior citizens should mark today also as a 'medal of honour' to their services, sacrifices, loyalties, and patriotism to their fatherland or wherever they must have served, but unfortunately even as I pen this, some sick and tired, dying, bedridden pensioners are on their ways returning from wherever they have gone to submit their 'papers'.

May Day has become a horror and a nightmare to pensioners as they reflect on their sufferings and hardships. Some of these hungry and aged senior citizens cry for over ninety month-pensions, arrears, and gratuities while some cry for more and or less.

Some are simply waiting to die, thank heavens who gave most of them children and other sources of livelihood.

However, I mourn for those ones who weren't lucky enough to either marry or have children, or the ones whose children are still in nursery schools, the ones without relatives or helpers, it is better unimagined...'woe unto them'.

What is the pensioner celebrating on a day like this, is it penury, is it mockery, is it shame, is it pain, is it sickness, is it anarchy, is it betrayal, is it wickedness, is it man's inhumanity to man, what is it??

These pensioners only needed to be paid their rights, their own monies, their own sweat, the greenness of their energy; something the living, the dead, the unborn, heaven, hell and earth know rightfully belongs to them.

These monies are not up to a looter's loot, nor a Stealer's steal, not up to their dog's breakfast, nor their concubine's freebie.... not upto the weeds for some thugs.

Happy Workers' Day to all pensioners all over the world, surely the labours of our heroes past shall never be in vain.
WELCOME TO MAY

THE WEB

Coronavirus was the pipe, a conduit one at that.

They announced a lockdown, just a lockdown. You are on your own.

They began to donate, a show of glamour for whatever, sane climes excluded.

And then came fire, fire and the fire.

So reared Isolation centers, crazy and funny ones.

Schools, especially the greedy pockets and pickpocketers started their own learning and teaching drama. The folks that destroyed public school.

And then came the Almighty palliatives, they gather thousands for one carton of indomie with high risks and chances of spreading diseases.
They shout and sing palliatives, deceiving the world whereas individuals were doing more sane and superb palliatives, even unannounced.

The relaxation, the curfew, the access, the burials, the carelessness, the jokes and the jokers; all lie on the same plain.

They have killed more people with bullets and hunger.

They lock down, they just lock down, nothing again, and the ravaging increases.

They copy and paste, without checking where, when, how, what, ...

A bunch of inhumane folks, undoing a nation. A company of aliens striping wombs and ripping off unborns.

If you think there is hell, think twice, I have seen one. Nigeria!
OUR PINNACLE

When we talk to people, they think we are talking about ourselves.

When we talk about ourselves, they think we are talking to people.

When we talk, they think we are talking to and about "them and ourselves"

When we talk, they hear our voices only,
When we write, they read our words only.

Confusion, misunderstanding, misinterpretation, misconception, and miswhatever.

Consult your Oracle, lest you fall from our pinnacle.

GOVERNMENT

If you tell me of war
And about crime,
If you tell me of deceit
And about greed,
If you tell me of terrorism
And its horrors,
If you tell me of evil
And about atrocity,
If you tell me of bizarre
And its nightmares,
Then I would assume
You are telling me of government.

LORD, I AM THINE!

Lord, confine me to your limits
Protect me in your bounds,
Shelter me under your tent
Direct me within your path
Lead me for your sake,
Anchor me throughout this life,
Burn the flame of my desire
Regulate my speed,
Drive my passion
Provide my needs
Pick my wants
Determine my pattern,
Fight my battle
Win my victory
And decide my end.

LORD, I AM THINE

THE CHANGE IN JUDAS

Genesis of lamentations
Exodus in numbers,
Chronicles of revelations
Changeful acts of apostles,

Judas has betrayed
Jesus, refused to die.

No fish, no bread
No manna, no miracle
The multitude wails.

Hypocrites mourn
Betrayers hang,
Jesus rules.

MEN OF NO VALOUR

Men of no valour
Strike in vain,
Steal the value
Darken the serene,
Dialogue behind the scene
Drama on the screen,
The game of shame
The lame still same.

THE NEGOTIATION TABLE

The negotiation table of an opaque glass prism,
The turn table of swinging pendulum,
The drawing board and logistics of dead issues, very dead on
arrival.
Merry, dance, a cup of coffee
Then the kiss of betrayal.
Jesus already knows he would die
Dying to save us,
Shame! He must resurrect
That day, the people will INVADE POWER
And the wall of Jericho will fall IN PERPETUITY

THE SWORD OF DIVORCE

Wedded by an alien
Married to a stranger,
I have forty children
And four hundred grandchildren,
He threatens divorce
But i never had a husband
Because i had been a monster,
Should he file for divorce?

HAPPY CHILDREN'S DAY

In a world where children bear the brunt of war, terrorism, religion, rituals, rape and all kinds of violence, is humanity still sacred?

In a world where children are legally aborted, sold and or bought, should we still celebrate them?

In homes where dads are butterflies and mums are promiscuous, or photo-dads and overstretched mums, what becomes the children's fate?

In a world where wrongs flush rights... we plant hate on our scarce fertile land and nurture love on our barren vast sea.

In a world where reality is fake.... we wear a frowning smile to mask our sadness.

In a world where the long claws of fate grab, hawk, traffic, rape and murder our children, who celebrates them?

By the way HAPPY CHILDREN'S DAY to my celebrities (nephews and nieces....including those on their way)....the world must celebrate you.

WE PRAY

Lord, we foil every plan of the enemy today and beyond. No weapon fashioned against us shall prosper. We break all the bows of the evil one.

No divination against Jacob and no enchantment against Israel for thy word is a lamp unto our feet and a light unto our path.

In whatever form, by whoever person, at wherever place, from however might, Lord we freeze their altar in perpetuity.

We take control of our vicinities, be they physical, spiritual, mental, social, cultural, local, national, international and whichever.

We decree and declare PEACE!
LORD, IT IS WELL WITH US AND OURS....AMEN!

DIAMOND GARDEN

Are you a gem or precious stone,
Do you dazzle or glitter?
Are you a star or moon,
Do you twinkle or illuminate?
Are you a sun or snow,
Do you shine or fall?
Are you a rainbow or heavenly body,
Do you signify or beautify?
Are you an alpha, a beta or gamma ray,
Do you emit light or radiate?
Are you incandescent or ultraviolet,
Are you multicoloured or multitalented?
Are you contagious or spontaneous,
Do you magnet or accelerate?
Are you a catalyst or heat
Do you bombard or react?
Do you fly or glow or boom or blossom?
Do you lift or motivate or fertilize or energize?
Do you anchor or mobilize or nourish or inspire?
Are you one, two, more or all of the above?
Join then the DIAMOND GARDEN, and grow your DIAMONDS.
I am a DIAMOND ROSE, what are you?

DIAMONDGARDEN.....A PLACE SOLELY FOR DIAMONDS

STAR

When my wallet mockingly say to me, 'Ngozi, you are not a star,
My mind confidently whispers 'Ngozi, you are a bank....a world
bank,
Then, proudly I respond 'dear wallet, if you think I want to be a
star, you obviously do not know the meaning of a star.

When i become a poet, i would start writing.
When i become a writer, i would be myself.
When i become myself, i would be a better seer.
When i see better, you would have me best.
FUNNY JOKE

Some get hundreds of millions when they threaten, upon killings
Some get buried for wanting to part.

Some are disenfranchised willfully, locally, geographically,
strategically,...for wanting to vote.

Some celebrate the peoples' government even when they are
sealed up.

Some faithfully Mann their defense.

Some solve algebra, permutations, differentiations, probabilities,
surd, quadratic equations, matrices and other further maths to
arrive at the future.

Some steal mace, some vomit dollar from the land of erehwon.

Some fall sick, some pretend, some uphold their allegiance,
alliance, alignment, secretly and openly.

Some scrap history, threatening fire and brimstone if revisited.

Some die of hunger, disease, ignorance, illiteracy, ...

Some trade and trample on skulls.

And some get excited to crack down.

Some amazing ones keep mute, the politically correct ones.

THE LAND IS RED

When your foods are gone
And your monies gone,
When your properties are gone
And your jobs gone,
When your children are gone
And your families gone,
When something dear is gone
Or everything lovely, gone
Then you would realize
It's been long we stopped being humans.

HELP!

Lots of psalms inspired,
Too weak to write.

Contrite,
Troubled pen.

Faint spirit,
Broken heart.

Feeble knees,
Shallow mind.

Hopeless, senseless
Helpless.

FALLOW FURROW

Fallow furrow, white and green

Rich and pure, great and lovely

Beautiful, wonderful and natural

But troubled, worried and bullied!

Fallow furrow, real and true

Neat, clean, spick and span

Green, booming, lively and humble

Yet, caged, sick and tired!

Fallow furrow, high and low

Rosy, nosy, windy and breezy

Still, crafty, cunning and moody!

Vegetations of delightful aura

Plantations of blissful wants and needs

Yet, still, but nature tires and retires!

Hindrances and obstructions

Nuisances and objections

Resistances and restrictions

Resonances and inscriptions

Fallow furrow; waiting long in emptiness!

Furrows of fallow boredom

Fallow furrows of terrible freedom

Whiling away time and chance

Rolling back tides and fortune

Staking life, gifts and Future!

About the Author

Ngozi Olivia Osuoha is a Nigerian graduate of Estate Management with experience in Banking and Broadcasting.

She has authored twenty three poetry books, and has featured in over one hundred and ten international anthologies. She has published over three hundred and twenty poems in over forty countries, and some of her pieces have been translated and published in Spanish, Polish, Russian, Romanian, Farsi, Arabic, Khloe, Serbian, Scots, Chinese, Hindi, Assamese, Macedonian, among others.

She has won several awards, and some of her works have been nominated for Pushcart Prize, Best of the Net Awards, and others.

She has some of her books in foreign libraries, including the US Library of Congress. She's a tailor too. And she has much more things to accomplish.